Anarchist
(S)Top Trump(s)

Pirate Press

ISBN: 198660764X

ISBN-13: 978-1986607643

HOW TO MAKE THE GAME

Ideally laminate each page.

Alternately you could stick card to the back of each sheet with a glue that will not come through to the front side or just use the paper.

Cut around each of the cards.

Cut and assemble the card box from the back cover using glue.

Buy more copies of the book for all your friends and relations.

HOW TO PLAY

Any number of people within reason can play. Shuffle and deal all the cards face down. Each player holds their cards so that they can see the top card only.

The player to the dealers left starts by reading out an item from the top card. The other players then read out the same item from their cards. The one with the highest value wins and places all of the top cards including their own to the bottom of their pile.

If two or more cards hold the same value then all the cards are placed in the middle and the same player chooses again from the next card. The winner of the hand takes the cards in the middle as well.

The person with all the cards at the end is the winner.

CONTENTS

Our respects go out to all these great anarchists both living and dead

Alexander Berkman 1870-1936
Ba Jin (Li Feigan) 1904-2005
Micheal Bakunin 1814-1876
Marie Louise Berneri 1918-1949
Murray Bookchin 1921-2006
Noam Chomsky 1928-
John Creaghe 1841-1920
Stuart Christie 1946-
Buenaventura Durruti 1896-1936
Ferdinand Domela Nieuwenhuis 1846-1919
Francisco Ferrer 1859-1909
William Godwin 1756-1836
Emma Goldman 1869-1940
Paul Goodman 1911-1972
Kotoku Shusui 1871-1911
Peter Kropotkin 1842-1921
Gustav Landauer 1870-1919
Ricardo Flores Magon 1874-1922
Nestor Makhno 1888-1934
Errico Malatesta 1853-1932
Albert Meltzer 1920-1996
Louise Michel 1830-1905
Federica Montseny 1905-1994
Johann Most 1846-1906
Lucy Parsons 1853?-1942
Rose Pesotta 1896-1965
Giuseppe Pinelli 1928-1969
Pierre-Joseph Proudhon 1809-1865
Elisee Reclus 1830-1905
Vernon Richards 1915-2001
Rudolf Rocker 1873-1958
Nicola Sacco 1891-1927 & Bartolomeo Vanzetti 1888-1927
Leo Tolstoy 1828-1910
B. Traven 1882?-1969
Colin Ward 1924-2010
Emiliano Zapata 1879-1919

Alexander Berkman

Amount Written	13
Beard Length	3
Age	66
Class Struggleness	20

Ba Jin (Li Feigan)

Amount Written	20
Beard Length	0
Age	100
Class Struggleness	12

Michael Bakunin

Amount Written	20
Beard Length	18
Age	62
Class Struggleness	20

Marie Louise Berneri

Amount Written	6
Beard Length	0
Age	31
Class Struggleness	20

Murray Bookchin

Amount Written	20
Beard Length	11
Age	85
Class Struggleness	15

Noam Chomsky

Amount Written	20
Beard Length	2
Age	89*
Class Struggleness	8

John Creaghe

Amount Written	10
Beard Length	15
Age	78
Class Struggleness	20

Stuart Christie

Amount Written	10
Beard Length	5
Age	71*
Class Struggleness	20

Buenaventura Durruti

Amount Written	6
Beard Length	2
Age	40
Class Struggleness	20

Ferdinand Domela Nieuwenhuis

Amount Written	20
Beard Length	18
Age	73
Class Struggleness	13

Francisco Ferrer

Amount Written	15
Beard Length	14
Age	50
Class Struggleness	18

William Godwin

Amount Written	10
Beard Length	2
Age	80
Class Struggleness	2

Emma Goldman

Amount Written	19
Beard Length	0
Age	71
Class Struggleness	19

Paul Goodman

Amount Written	20
Beard Length	3
Age	61
Class Struggleness	3

Kotoku Shusui

Amount Written	16
Beard Length	6
Age	39
Class Struggleness	15

Peter Kropotkin

Amount Written	20
Beard Length	20
Age	78
Class Struggleness	13

Gustav Landauer

Amount Written 13
Beard Length 17
Age 49
Class Struggleness 14

Ricardo Flores Magon

Amount Written 12
Beard Length 6
Age 48
Class Struggleness 17

Nestor Makhno

Amount Written 6
Beard Length 7
Age 45
Class Struggleness 20

Errico Malatesta

Amount Written 10
Beard Length 8
Age 78
Class Struggleness 20

Albert Meltzer

Amount Written	5
Beard Length	4
Age	76
Class Struggleness	20

Louise Michel

Amount Written	11
Beard Length	0
Age	74
Class Struggleness	20

Federica Montseny

Amount Written	17
Beard Length	0
Age	88
Class Struggleness	20

Johann Most

Amount Written	14
Beard Length	17
Age	60
Class Struggleness	19

Lucy Parsons

Amount Written	13
Beard Length	0
Age	89
Class Struggleness	20

Rose Pesotta

Amount Written	5
Beard Length	0
Age	69
Class Struggleness	16

Guiseppe Pinelli

Amount Written	4
Beard Length	12
Age	41
Class Struggleness	19

Pierre-Joseph Proudhon

Amount Written	11
Beard Length	15
Age	56
Class Struggleness	3

Elisee Reclus

Amount Written	14
Beard Length	15
Age	75
Class Struggleness	17

Vernon Richards

Amount Written	12
Beard Length	5
Age	86
Class Struggleness	14

Rudolf Rocker

Amount Written	16
Beard Length	7
Age	85
Class Struggleness	19

Leo Tolstoy

Amount Written	17
Beard Length	20
Age	82
Class Struggleness	5

B. Traven

Amount Written	15
Beard Length	2
Age	87
Class Struggleness	15

Nicola Sacco & Bartolomeo Vanzetti

Amount Written	3
Beard Length	6
Average Age	48
Class Struggleness	19

Colin Ward

Amount Written	19
Beard Length	3
Age	86
Class Struggleness	10

Emiliano Zapata

Amount Written	2
Beard Length	7
Age	39
Class Struggleness	17